ECOLOGY ALERT!

Energy

Jane Featherstone

RAINTREE
STECK-VAUGHN
PUBLISHERS
A Steck-Vaughn Company

Austin, Texas

Ecology Alert!

Coasts   Farming

Communities   Transportation

Energy   Rivers

Cover: Welding metal gives off a shower of sparks.

Title page: Traffic and neon signs in Hong Kong

Contents page: Wind provides energy for a turbine and a sailboat.

Published by Raintree Steck-Vaughn Publishers, an imprint of Steck-Vaughn Company

Library of Congress Cataloging-in-Publication Data
Featherstone, Jane.
Energy / Jane Featherstone.
     p.   cm.—(Ecology Alert)
Includes bibliographical references and index.
Summary: Discusses energy, its uses and effects on the environment, and describes renewable energy sources such as solar, wind, and geothermal power. Includes case studies and activities.
ISBN 0-8172-5374-2
1. Power resources—Juvenile literature.
2. Environmental protection—Juvenile literature.
[1. Power resources.]
I. Title. II. Series.
TJ163.23.F43 1999
333.79—dc21   98-34740

Printed in Italy. Bound in the United States.
1 2 3 4 5 6 7 8 9 0 03 02 01 00 99

Picture acknowledgments
Axiom Photographic Agency (Jim Holmes) 20, (Jim Holmes) 28; James Davis Travel Photography 3; Ecoscene (Angela Hampton) 18, (Nick Hawkes) 25; Eye Ubiquitous 4 bottom; Impact Photos (Mark Henley) 1, (Tony Page) 5, (Jorn Stjerneklar) 8 bottom, (Homer Sykes) 9, (Yann Arthus Betrand) 10, (Peter Arkell) 11, (Charles Coates) 16, (Mark Henley) 19, (Javed A Jaferji) 22; W. Lord 26; Sheffield City Council 23 both; Splash Communications 21 both; Tony Stone Images (Terry Vine) cover, (David Young Wolff) 4 top, (Mike Abrahams) 7, (Ken Graham) 13, (Tony Craddock) 17 top, (Dave Jacobs) 24; Trip (M Watson) 14; Wayland Picture Library 6, 8 top, 12, 17 bottom, 27.
Artwork by Peter Bull Art Studio.

Contents

Your Life and Energy

You got up this morning. Perhaps an alarm clock went off, or you turned on the radio. You may have switched on the light. If you live in a cold climate, your bedroom was probably warm because you have heating.

What did you do next? Did you go to the bathroom, have a hot shower? Did you then have some breakfast? Were you listening to the radio or watching television?

By then it must have been time to go to school. Did someone take you in a car, or did you go by train or bus? When you arrived at school, the heating may have been on for several hours, and the lights were burning in your classroom. Classes started. Was it your turn to work on the computer?

We do all these things nearly every day. We do not think about it much, but everything we do uses energy. Everything we eat or use has needed energy to make it. It took energy to light your home and get you to school. It took energy to heat your water, to bake your bread, and to make your clothes. We use an enormous amount of energy.

▲ Machines that use energy are needed for many household tasks.

▶ Computers at home and in schools, factories, and offices also use energy.

Where does all this energy come from? How much do we use? Does everyone have enough? How is it made? Are some ways of making energy better than others? Does making it or using it harm the environment? Does this matter? Does it matter how much energy you use?

Yes, it does! Many people think that the ways we make energy and the amounts of energy we use are seriously damaging the environment.

This book will help you understand some of these problems. It may help you decide for yourself whether you need to change your lifestyle in order to conserve resources and protect the environment.

Oil refineries and power plants give off gases and smoke that can cause serious air pollution.

Activity

Energy diary

Think about how and where you use energy. Make a diary of everything you have done today so far.

Time	What I did	What energy was used for	Form of energy

Look at the inside and outside of your home. What types of energy does it use? Where does the energy come in? How is it used?

Sources of Energy

Living things, that is, plants, animals, and people, get energy from food. Animals and people need energy to stay alive and to do things such as moving around and finding food. People also use energy from natural resources to run machines that do work for us and to provide heat and light.

Energy comes from sources that are either renewable or non-renewable.
• Renewable sources, such as wind, sun, or water, will not run out.
• Nonrenewable sources, such as coal, oil, natural gas, and uranium, will run out and cannot be replaced.

Where does this energy come from?

Energy comes from a variety of sources. Some comes from burning wood, coal, oil, or gas. These are all called fuels. Some comes from the power of falling or moving water. Even more is made as nuclear power, using the metal uranium.

Energy can come from the body or from fuels used to power machines.

Other sources of energy are the wind or the sun. These are called renewable sources of energy and are discussed in the last chapter.

Wood

Throughout human history, burning wood has been the main source of energy. In many countries, it is still the most common fuel for cooking and heating. It is known as fuelwood.

Fossil fuels

During the eighteenth and nineteenth centuries, people discovered how to burn coal, oil, and natural gas to produce energy. These are called fossil fuels. They are made from the fossilized remains of plants and animals.

Some coal mines are a long way underground. Others are on the surface of the land.

Coal is formed from the remains of trees, ferns, and other plants. When the plants died, thick layers built up over many thousands of years. Eventually, these layers were squeezed together and made coal. Oil and gas were made from plants and animals that lived and died in the sea. Bacteria, heat from the earth, and the weight of rock above slowly changed the remains into oil and natural gas.

Coal, oil, and gas are nonrenewable fuels because they cannot be replaced in human time scales. They take millions of years to form. Burning these fuels makes new materials, such as gas, ash, and smoke. These are waste products and can cause pollution.

Water power

Moving water can be another source of energy. In order to use the energy, water must be flowing from a higher place to a lower place. To collect water in a high place, a dam is built across a river. The water collects behind the dam in a large lake, called a reservoir. A power house is built in or near the dam. The water flows downward through turbines that turn the energy into electricity.

Electricity made with water power is clean power. That is because no harmful gases are made and there is no waste.

▲ To extract oil from the ground, very deep holes are made with huge metal drills.

▼ Water flowing from a higher place to a lower place has plenty of energy.

Competing for oil around the Caspian Sea

Huge amounts of oil exist under the Caspian Sea. This is a large landlocked sea, bordered by Russia, Kazakhstan, Turkmenistan, Iran, and Azerbaijan.

Unfortunately, these countries do not get along with one another. They argue over who owns the vast amounts of oil. This field is thought to be the last large oil field to be used in the world. It may contain 100 billion barrels of oil. (One barrel of oil equals 42 gal. [159 l].)

The countries around the Caspian Sea may agree to divide the seabed and share the oil that lies beneath it. The next problem is how to transport the oil. At the moment all the pipelines go across Russia. European and American oil companies want to build oil wells. Pipelines will have to be built across many countries so that the oil can be sold in Europe, the Americas, or Asia.

Many of the countries around the Caspian Sea have been at war with each other in the last few years. Some people think that more wars could break out because of the oil, since it is such an important source of energy.

To drill for oil under water, oil rigs are built and anchored in the sea. They are huge, often the size of small towns.

Nuclear power

In 1937, two German scientists found that atoms of uranium can release enormous amounts of energy if they are split apart. At first, this energy was used in bombs that the United States dropped on Japan to end World War II. Scientists later worked out a way of controlling the energy in power plants, to make electricity.

Many people are afraid that nuclear power is not safe. Nuclear reactions give off radioactivity, which damages living things. The uranium fuel must be used and stored very carefully, because it can harm fish, animals, and people.

The core of a nuclear power plant in France

Changes in use of energy (U.S.)

1850
Wood 80%, Coal 20%

1990
Oil 46%, Coal 28%, Gas 19%
Nuclear and water power 7%

Turning energy into electricity

Electricity is not a source of energy. Electricity has to be made. It is a form of energy that is easy for people to use. There are different ways to generate, or make, electricity. It can be generated in hydroelectric power plants, which use the power of falling water to turn the generators. Coal, gas, oil, or nuclear-powered plants produce heat to make steam, which can also turn the generators.

Energy around the world

Coal, natural gas, and oil are not found in all countries of the world. Two-thirds of the world's fossil fuels are found in industrialized countries, although they have a only quarter of the world's population.

A country that has the resources to make energy is in a powerful position because it can manufacture goods, run a transportation system, and supply the energy that people want. Some countries have so much coal, oil, or gas, they can sell it to other countries, which helps them grow rich.

Many countries are not able to provide the energy their people need to have a good quality of life. These countries have no fossil fuels from which to make energy. They rely on wood for fuel. Other countries borrow money to build hydroelectric power plants to make use of their rivers to provide power.

A car production line. Countries with energy can make goods like this to sell.

Activity

Where does your energy come from?

Find out what sources of fuel are used in your region. You may be able to find this out by contacting your electricity or gas supplier. Make a map of the area to show the location of:

- Coal mines or gas or oil fields.
- Power plants that burn coal, gas, or oil.
- Hydroelectric power plants.
- Nuclear power plants.

Energy and the Environment

Does making energy harm the environment? Are some ways of making energy better than others?

Producing energy or generating electricity can be harmful in different ways.

1 Using up the earth's resources

When coal, oil, and gas are used as fuels, the earth's resources are being used up.

2 Extracting the earth's resources

Mining for coal involves digging a vast network of tunnels under the ground or creating large pits. When the coal has been extracted, huge piles of waste, called slag, are left over. When the mine is abandoned, the land is left scarred, and there may be erosion. It costs a great deal of money to make the land usable again.

Supplies of nonrenewable resources

If we continue to use fossil fuels at the same rate as now, they will eventually run out. Here is an estimate of how long they may last:

Black coal	190 years
Brown coal	300 years
Oil	45 years
Natural Gas	65 years

An open-face coal mine in Germany, with a power plant behind it

When oil rigs are no longer needed, it is very difficult to know what to do with them because they are enormous and often contain large quantities of harmful chemicals.

3 Transporting fuels

Moving the fuel from one place to another can damage the environment. Many fuels are moved in trucks that produce fumes causing air pollution and that use up even more energy. Oil pipelines leak, and tankers spill oil at sea. These pollute water and soil, damage beaches, and kill wildlife.

Oil is transported over long distances in pipes. This pipeline crosses Alaska.

4 Making energy

Coal-, gas-, and oil-fired power plants release gases that pollute the air. Nuclear waste can be dangerous for thousands of years after it is produced, and no one can find a safe way to store it or get rid of it.

Dams are built for hydroelectricity. They block rivers, flood surrounding land, and sometimes force large numbers of people to move.

13

The Three Gorges project

China is the world's second largest producer of coal. But it has such a large population that most people have to use animal or human power for transportation or to do jobs such as plowing fields.

A model of the Three Gorges Dam, in China, that shows what it will be like when it is built

In China a new dam is being built on the Yangtze River, the longest river in China.

The dam will be used to generate hydroelectricity. Enough electricity will be made to meet one-eighth of China's needs. This will save 45 million tons of coal each year. It will also avoid releasing huge amounts of polluting gases into the air.

However, building a dam has a huge environmental impact in the place where it is built. The reservoir will flood the Three Gorges, some of China's most spectacular scenery. The reservoir made by the dam will be 367 mi. (590 km) long. It will cover 9,700 acres (25,000 ha) of land, 13 cities, 140 towns, and hundreds of small villages. Many creatures that live in the river will lose their habitats. Two million people will have to find new homes.

Many people are against the dam's being built because of the effect it will have on their lives and on the environment. Dai Qing is a journalist. She spent ten months in prison because she wrote a book in protest against the dam. Thirty thousand copies of the book were destroyed by the government. She has said, "If the Three Gorges could speak, they would beg for mercy!"

5 Using energy

The use of gasoline, oil, coal, and natural gas produces the gas, carbon dioxide, which is linked to climate change and produces sulfur and nitrogen oxides, which cause acid rain.

Global warming and climate change

Many scientists are afraid that the burning of increasing amounts of fossil fuels may be changing the whole pattern of the earth's climate.

The earth is surrounded by a blanket of gases. These include water vapor, carbon dioxide, and methane. They trap heat near the surface—heat that would otherwise escape into space.

Without this layer of gases, the earth would be a frozen, lifeless planet. They are called greenhouse gases, because they trap heat near the earth in the same way that heat is trapped inside a greenhouse.

Greenhouse gases trap the warmth of the sun near the surface of the earth.

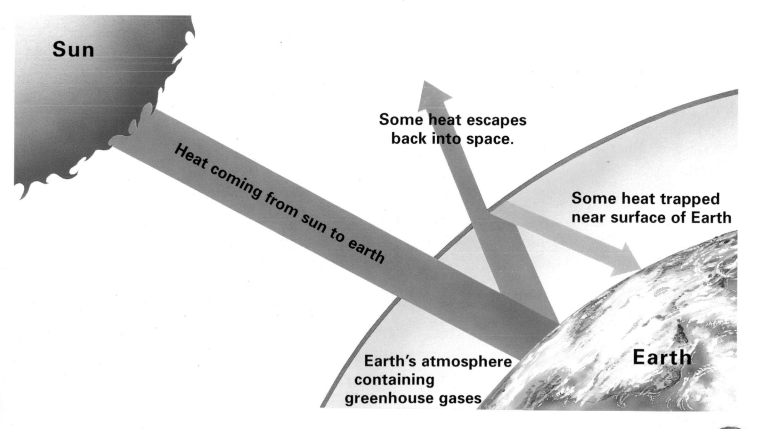

Sun

Heat coming from sun to earth

Some heat escapes back into space.

Some heat trapped near surface of Earth

Earth's atmosphere containing greenhouse gases

Earth

However, more of these gases are being released into the atmosphere. This is mainly due to the burning of fossil fuels, but the gases are also released by farm animals and by the destruction of forests. This is making the surface of the earth warmer and resulting in changes in climate all over the world.

The effects of global warming

Global warming may affect different places in different ways. Some places may get hotter and drier, but others may become cooler and wetter. The higher temperatures would melt the huge areas of ice at the North and South poles. Sea levels may rise 20 in. (50 cm) by the year 2100, flooding coastal zones and completely covering some small islands. At the same time, there may be a shortage of water in some countries.

Global warming may make some places hotter and drier.

Farming will be affected in such a way that less food can be grown. Many people may die in heat waves, and serious diseases, such as malaria, may spread to new areas. All over the world, many species of plants and animals may die out because they cannot adapt quickly enough to changes in their habitats.

Acid rain

Acid rain, sleet, and snow are made when sulfur and nitrogen oxides get into the atmosphere. The gases come mainly from power plants and from car exhausts. Coal-powered plants make the most pollution.

The gases mix with water to form weak acid. Wind blows the acid-bearing rain clouds over a wide area. The clouds release acid rain, often hundreds of miles away from the power plant. The acid rain destroys life in rivers and lakes and kills trees in forests.

◀ **Trees are killed by acid rain.**

Activity

▼ **Lichen on a tree trunk. Lichen can be green, gray, yellow, or brown.**

Lichen survey for air pollution

How polluted is the air near you? One way to find out is to carry out a lichen survey. Lichen is a type of plant that is very sensitive to air pollution. A good place to spot lichen is on the trunks of trees, rocks, walls, or roofs.

Find some lichen growing on tree trunks. You may find that there is lichen on one side but not on the other. This may mean the wind is blowing air pollution onto the bare side. Look in that direction and see if you can identify the source of pollution. It may be smoke from a chimney or fumes from cars on a road.

Using Energy

How much energy do we use? It is easy to find out how much energy we use at home and in school. Energy has to be paid for, so it is measured.

Activity

Exploring energy in your school

Find out where and how your school uses energy. You should:

- Make a list of every piece of equipment that uses energy.
- Find out where energy comes into school.
- Find out how the energy flows around the school.
- Find out where the controls and settings are.
- Find out where the meters are and what they are metering.

Measuring energy

The companies that supply you with energy, such as electricity, gas, or oil, need to know how much you use. There is a meter in every house and school that shows how much energy you have used. This might be a gas or electricity meter or a gauge on an oil tank. You can learn to read the meter.

People in the developed world use much more energy than people in developing countries.

Energy use around the world

Different countries use different amounts of energy. Although the countries of the developed world have only a quarter of the world's population, they use much more energy than all the people in developing countries.

Does energy use matter?

The more energy we use, the more quickly the earth's resources will be used up. The more energy we use, the more environmental damage there will be.

Rush hour in Calcutta, India. All over the world, traffic exhaust releases greenhouse gases into the atmosphere.

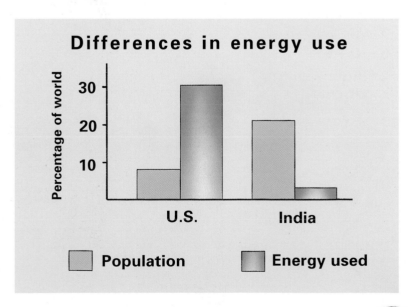

Differences in energy use

Percentage of world

30
20
10

U.S.   India

☐ **Population**   ☐ **Energy used**

Not enough energy

In many countries, people still rely on fuelwood for energy to cook food. Two billion people around the world are suffering from an energy crisis: that is, lack of fuelwood. They get the wood by cutting down trees.

Some people spend many hours a day collecting wood. Sometimes they have to walk a long way to find enough for their needs. Then they must carry it back home.

In some places, all the trees near a village have been cut down. This leads to soil erosion. People are having to use the dung from animals as fuel instead of putting it on the soil as fertilizer.

Even in a country with plenty of energy, such as the United States or the UK, there are people who die of cold every year because they cannot afford to heat their homes.

A woman in Bangladesh puts cow manure on sticks to use as fuel.

The Freeplay clockwork radio

Most people who use radios plug them into the electricity supply or use batteries. Batteries contain chemicals that release energy, but they are expensive. When the chemicals are used up, the batteries are usually thrown away. The chemicals can cause pollution.

An inventor named Trevor Baylis had a new idea when he heard about the spread of AIDS in Africa. He realized that many people around the world need to receive information about how to avoid catching this serious disease. One way to spread information, especially in the countryside, is by radio. However, many people cannot afford batteries or do not have electricity.

So Trevor Baylis invented a radio that does not need electricity or batteries. Instead, it works by clockwork, using body power. Energy is stored by winding a metal spring. When the spring is released it powers a generator. It takes about 20 seconds to wind the radio, which plays for up to an hour.

▲ The radio is powered by turning a handle that winds the spring inside.

◀ Freeplay radios are made in South Africa and sold all over the world.

Using Less Energy

The number of people in the world is increasing all the time. People are using more and more machines that use energy, such as cars, refrigerators, dishwashers, and air conditioners. How can we meet the ever greater needs of a growing world population?

Many people in the world do not have modern machines in their homes, but they would like to have them.

Using less energy

We can all think of ways to use less energy at home or at school. For example, switch off lights that are not needed. Switch off machines that are on standby, such as computers, photocopiers, and television sets. Turn down thermostats on radiators and water heaters.

Using energy more efficiently

We can also use energy more efficiently. For example, insulation in the roofs of buildings keeps heat from being lost. So does fitting draft excluders on doors and windows. New buildings can be designed with energy efficiency in mind.

Energy and governments

Governments can help by having a policy on energy. They can encourage people to use less energy and to use energy more efficiently. They can also persuade energy producers to use renewable sources. Governments can do this by putting an energy tax on homes and industry. The tax would be based on the amount of energy used, making energy more expensive. Governments can also support public transportation such as trains and buses, rather than private cars. They can encourage industry to recover as much energy as possible from waste.

CASE STUDY

The Green Heat Network

The "green heat" project is located in Sheffield, England. It works by burning the city's trash. The heat from burning the trash is not wasted by going up a chimney into the atmosphere. Instead, steam produced from burning the trash is made into hot water.

This hot water is pumped through underground pipes to buildings of all types in the city center, such as apartments, hospitals, offices, and theaters. The hot water is used to heat the buildings and to provide hot water itself. The steam produced from burning trash is also used to make electricity, which is sent into the local electricity supply.

This is a very environmentally friendly way of providing heat and power. Burning trash means that less has to be buried in the ground. Because trash is used as a fuel, less fossil fuel is used. Every year, the "green heat" project prevents more than 40,000 tons of carbon dioxide, a major greenhouse gas, from being released into the atmosphere.

▼ Trash is carried on a belt into an incinerator, where it is burned.

▶ Laying the pipeline that will carry hot water to Sheffield's city center

23

Renewable Energy

We now know that it is important to think about which energy sources to use and how much energy to use.

In most industrialized countries, such as the United States, Canada, and the UK, 95 percent of the energy comes from nonrenewable fossil fuels: that is, oil, coal, and natural gas.

We know that the use of fossil fuels harms the environment. We also know that fossil fuels are running out. As the demand for energy keeps growing, we must think about using energy efficiently and about using renewable energy sources.

Dishes that collect energy from the sun in Australia

Other sources of energy

There are many sources of energy that do less harm to the environment than using nonrenewable fossil fuels.

These sources of energy are called renewable sources:
- Wind power: using the flow of air to turn turbines.
- Wave power: using the energy of waves to turn turbines.
- Tidal power: using the flow of the tide in a river estuary to turn turbines.
- Solar power: using the direct heat of the sun.
- Geothermal power: using the heat in rocks far underground to heat water.
- Power from biomass: burning wood from trees grown for this purpose (such as willow), or burning straw from crops (such as wheat).
- Power from domestic waste: burning trash.

The tidal barrage on the Rance River, in France. Turbines inside this building use the energy of the tides going in and out to generate electricity.

Solar house

Bill and Debbi Lord's house, on the coast of Maine, produces its own heat, hot water, and electricity from the sun.

The glass roof of this solar-powered house faces south because that is where it gets the most sunlight.

The south-facing roof is covered with solar collectors under sheets of glass. There are two types of solar panels: one for heating water and another for producing electricity. The water circulates through the house and is used for hot water and heating.

The Lords have an unusual arrangement with the local suppliers of electricity, Central Maine Power. At night, and when there is no sun, the Lords get power from the electric company, which they pay for. However, when it is sunny, the house produces plenty of power. Whatever is not needed is sent to the electric company, and the Lords are paid for it.

The house also has excellent insulation, special insulated windows, and a ventilation system that lets air go out but keeps the heat in.

Bill Lord is so happy with his solar house that he has put an information page on the Internet's World Wide Web, describing how the house works and spreading his enthusiasm about solar living. (See page 31.)

Alternative energy and the environment

Even these sources of energy have an impact on the environment. To get energy from the tides, a barrage must be built across an estuary, but this damages habitats for wildlife. Geothermal energy requires drilling into rocks, destroying natural land. To gather solar energy on a large scale, vast areas of solar panels must be built.

What is good about renewable energy sources is that they do not produce harmful greenhouse gases.

Is nature's energy free?

Even though the source of power may be free, it is sometimes rather weak and not very reliable. Also, the machinery to use the power and to turn it into electricity may cost a lot of money to build.

Wind turbines can be an eyesore as well as being noisy.

In the United States, people use about 250 terawatt (TW) hours (250,000,000,000 kilowatts or units) of electricity a year. The Department of Energy thinks that some electricity might be from renewable sources by the year 2025.

	TW hours per year
Wind power	30
Tidal energy	28
Geothermal energy	10
Wave power	0.2
Small-scale hydro power	0.7

What about the future?

Many developing countries do not have large resources of fossil fuels. People there will have to use lots of different ways to make energy. The use of renewable energy sources will be very important for developing countries. Many of them are already building water-power plants.

In industrialized countries, people have depended on nonrenewable fuel sources. This cannot continue forever, so renewable energy will become increasingly important.

Solar power is a vital source of energy at a hospital in Tanzania.

Many people in industrialized countries are able to choose from which company to buy their electricity and gas. Perhaps they will choose companies that make their energy from alternative energy sources.

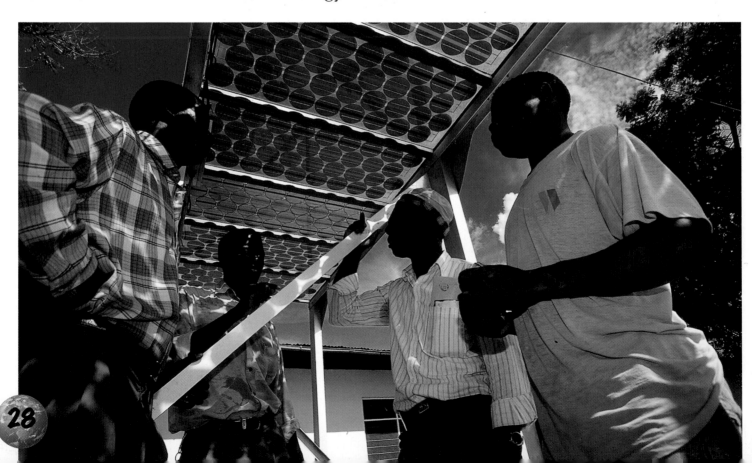

Activity

Make a solar panel

Try solar heating for yourself. You will need:
- Clear flexible PVC tubing, about $3/8$ in. (8mm) diameter
- 2 shallow cardboard containers, such as box lids
- Thin flexible wire, such as single-core electric wire
- Aluminum foil
- Black plastic garbage bag
- Plastic modeling clay
- Wire cutters, scissors, tape

1 Line one box lid with aluminum foil and the other with black plastic. Attach the linings on the box lids with tape.
2 Cut two pieces of tubing, about three times the length of the box lids.
3 Attach a piece of tubing onto each lid in an S shape, using small pieces of wire to hold them in place.
4 Put a small ball of modeling clay on one end of the tubing, fill the tube with water, and then put clay on the other end.
5 Place your solar panels outside where they will get the sun at midday. Leave the panels in the sun for a few hours.
6 Let the water run out of your panels into bowls. Is the water warm? Which solar panel works best, and why?

What kind of weather would a country need to have for solar power to be useful? Would it be useful in your country?

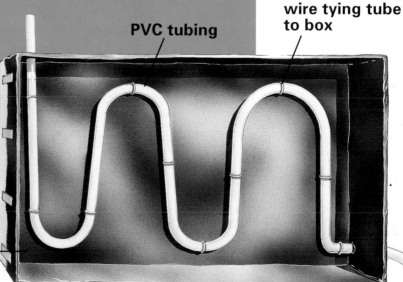

wire tying tube to box

PVC tubing

box lid

lining

Glossary

Acid rain   Rain containing pollution from vehicles and industry.

Bacteria   Tiny single-celled organisms that often cause diseases.

Dam   A wall built to hold back water.

Developed countries   Those where most people live in good conditions.

Developing countries   Poor countries that are developing better conditions for their people.

Environment   Everything in our surroundings: the earth, air, and water.

Erosion   Wearing away of the earth's surface.

Estuary   The mouth of a river at the sea where freshwater meets seawater.

Fossil fuel   Oil, coal, and natural gas, which were formed from the fossilized remains of plants and animals.

Fuel   Something that can be burned to give energy.

Generate   To make or produce electricity, light, or heat.

Greenhouse gases   Gases that trap the sun's heat close to the earth's surface.

Habitat   The natural home of a plant or animal.

Industrial   Having to do with making or manufacturing goods, usually by machines in factories.

Industrialized country   A country that earns most of its money from industries.

Insulation   A material that does not let heat (or electricity) through easily.

Nonrenewable   Something that cannot be replaced is nonrenewable.

Pollution   Damage to air, water, or land by harmful materials.

Population   The number of people who live in a place.

Radioactive   Giving out radiation or particles.

Renewable   Something that will not run out or that can be replaced.

Reservoir   An artificial lake made to store a large amount of water.

Resources   Things that humans use to survive or to improve their lives.

Solar   Having to do with the sun.

Species   A group of plants or animals with similar features.

Tides   The rise and fall of the sea on the shore.

Turbine   A machine powered by steam, gas, or water that can generate electricity.

Waste   Trash and garbage; things that are not needed or are unusable.

Further Information

Books

Challoner, Jack. *Energy* (Eyewitness Science). New York: Dorling Kindersley Publishing, 1993.

Doherty, Paul and Don Rathjen. *The Cool Hot Rod and Other Electrifying Experiments of Energy and Matter* (Exploratorium Science Snackbook). New York: John Wiley & Sons, 1996.

Hawkes, Nigel. *Energy* (New Technology). New York: 21st Century Books, 1995.

Jennings, Terry J. *Finding Out About Energy* (Making Science Work). Austin, TX: Raintree Steck-Vaughn, 1996.

Parker, Steve. *Fuels for the Future* (Protecting Our Planet). Austin, TX: Raintree Steck-Vaughn, 1998.

Snedden, Robert. *Energy* (Science Horizons). New York: Chelsea House, 1995.

Woodruff, John. *Energy* (Science Projects). Austin, TX: Raintree Steck-Vaughn, 1998.

Internet sites

The Lord solar house web site can be found at:
http://solstice.crest.org/renewables/wlord/index.html

Index